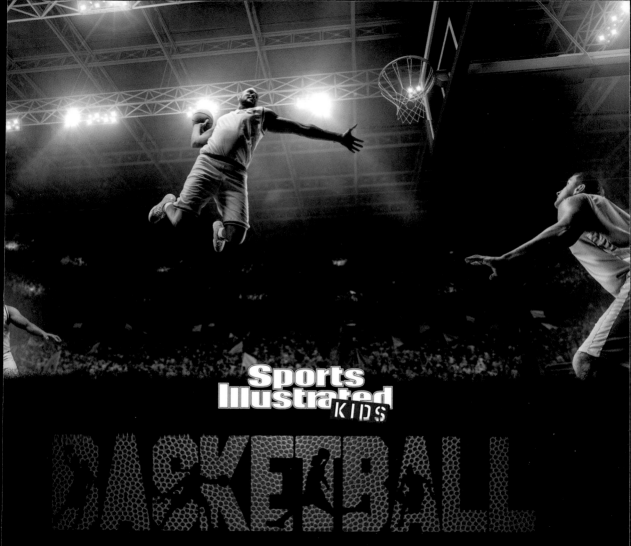

Sports Illustrated KIDS

BASKETBALL

GREATS

Capstone Captivate is published by Capstone Press, an imprint of Capstone.
1710 Roe Crest Drive
North Mankato, Minnesota 56003
www.capstonepub.com
SPORTS ILLUSTRATED KIDS is a trademark of ABG-SI LLC. Used with permission.

Library of Congress Cataloging-in-Publication Data
Names: Doeden, Matt, author.
Title: Basketball greats / by Matt Doeden.
Description: North Mankato, Minnesota : Capstone Captivate is published by
Capstone Press, [2022] | Series: Sports Illustrated Kids: Ball |
Includes webography. | Includes bibliographical references and index. |
Audience: Ages 8-11 years | Audience: Grades 4-6 | Summary: "How did pro
basketball biggest stars become the greatest players of all time? By playing the game in ways no one had ever done before! Discover the magic that propelled players like Julius "Dr. J" Irving, Michael Jordan, LeBron James, Maya Moore, and others to superstardom"-- Provided by publisher.
Identifiers: LCCN 2021015954 (print) | LCCN 2021015955 (ebook) | ISBN 9781663906632 (Hardcover) | ISBN 9781663920713 (Paperback) | ISBN 9781663906601 (PDF) | ISBN 9781663906625 (Kindle Edition) Subjects: LCSH: Basketball players--Juvenile literature.
| Women basketball players--Juvenile literature. | Basketball players--Rating of--Juvenile literature. | Basketball--Records--Juvenile literature. | Basketball--History--Juvenile literature. | National Basketball Association--History. | Women's National Basketball Association--History.
Classification: LCC GV885.1 .D629 2022 (print) | LCC GV885.1 (ebook) | DDC 796.323092/2--dc23 LC record available at https://lccn.loc.gov/2021015954 LC ebook record available at https://lccn.loc.gov/2021015955

Image Credits
Associated Press: Alvin Chung, 9, AP Photo, 22, Dave Tenenbaum, 8, Jeff Haldiman, 29, Pat Sullivan, 21, Stuart Ramson, 27; Shutterstock: Africa Studio, (writing) design element, Alex Kravtsov, 1, Chamnong Inthasaro, (court) design element, ChromaCo, (silhouette) Cover, Dan Thornberg, (ball texture) Cover, EFKS, (arena) Cover, Stephen Marques, (court lines) Cover, SvgOcean, (basketball word) Cover, teka12, (girl) Cover; Sports Illustrated: Al Tielemans, 5, Bill Frakes, 28, John Biever, 26, John G. Zimmerman, 7, John W. McDonough, 14, Manny Millan, 10, 17, 18, 19, 20, 24, 25, Neil Leifer, 13, Peter Read Miller, bottom Cover, 11, Robert Beck, 12

TABLE OF CONTENTS

Words in **bold** are in the glossary.

BIG SPOT SHOT

The clock is ticking. It's a tie game in overtime. Steph Curry hurries the ball up the court. Three seconds remain . . . two seconds. Curry rises and launches a shot from deep. The ball sails through the air. Swish! Game over!

Curry is one in a long line of National Basketball Association (NBA) and Women's National Basketball Association (WNBA) legends. Their shot-making, passing, and defense have changed the way the game is played.

Sharpshooter Steph Curry rises up to take a shot in the 2015 NBA All-Star Game.

CHAPTER 1

GAME-CHANGERS

There are greats. And then there are game-changers. These are the players who altered the game itself.

Wilt Chamberlain

One of the first game-changers was center Wilt Chamberlain. He was 7 feet, 1 inch tall (216 centimeters). He towered over opponents. Chamberlain was a wrecking ball down low. He had power and **agility**, and he was willing to fight for the ball.

The NBA passed new rules just to slow down Chamberlain. They widened the lane near the basket. Players can pass through this area. But they can't stay there. The league was doing all it could to slow down Chamberlain's dominance.

Wilt Chamberlain leaps for a rebound in a game against the Boston Celtics.

Cheryl Miller (center) celebrates her Olympic gold medal with her parents in 1984.

DID YOU KNOW?

Basketball skills ran in Miller's family. Her younger brother, Reggie, also played. He was a Hall of Fame guard for the NBA's Indiana Pacers.

Cheryl Miller

The women's game really began to take off in the 1980s. Cheryl Miller was a big reason. Miller was an amazing athlete with a sweet shot. She led the University of Southern California to championships in 1983 and 1984. She also won a gold medal with the U.S. team at the 1984 Olympics.

Miller was even **drafted** into the men's United States Basketball League. But knee injuries cut her career short. Fans can only wonder how much more she might have done if she had stayed healthy.

Cheryl Miller (#31) plays in a game against UCLA.

Kevin Garnett and Kobe Bryant

Until the mid-1990s, players usually didn't go straight from high school to the pros. But in 1995, high schooler Kevin Garnett changed that. The Minnesota Timberwolves selected him with the fifth pick in the **draft**. Garnett was a great athlete and a terror on defense.

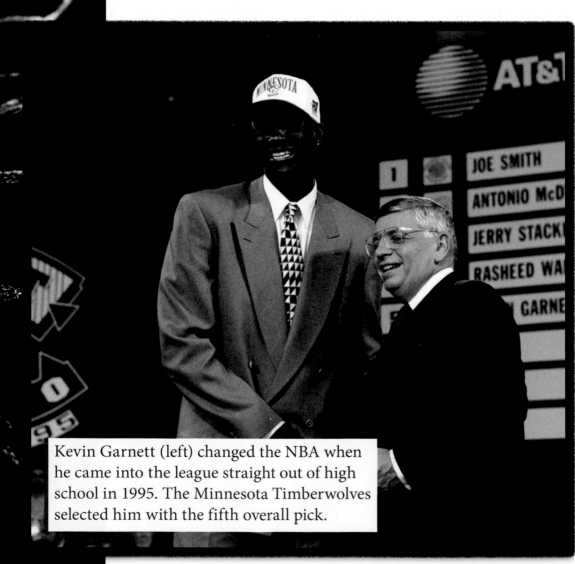

Kevin Garnett (left) changed the NBA when he came into the league straight out of high school in 1995. The Minnesota Timberwolves selected him with the fifth overall pick.

Kobe Bryant (holding trophy) celebrates the 2010 NBA championship with his Lakers teammates.

A year later, Kobe Bryant followed in his footsteps. Bryant ended up with the Los Angeles Lakers. Bryant became one of the game's all-time **clutch** shooters. He won five NBA titles with the Lakers.

Dirk Nowitzki

In 1998, the Dallas Mavericks acquired German forward Dirk Nowitzki. At the time, few NBA players came from overseas. Many fans thought European players were not star-level players.

Nowitzki stood 7 feet (2.13 m) tall. He had great ball skills and a deadly shooting touch. Nowitzki changed the way people thought about European players. He also set a new standard in how big men could attack from the outside. He was the 2007 Most Valuable Player (MVP). He led Dallas to a championship in 2011.

Dirk Nowitzki (right) uses his long arms to defend the Lakers' Gary Payton.

The 1992 Dream Team included (left to right) Larry Bird, Michael Jordan, and Magic Johnson.

THE DREAM TEAM

Many experts credit the 1992 U.S. Men's Olympic team with helping to kickstart **international** interest in the game. The "Dream Team" included 11 future Hall of Famers. They included Michael Jordan, Magic Johnson, Larry Bird, and Charles Barkley. The team cruised to gold at the games in Barcelona. They thrilled fans with every pass, shot, and slam dunk.

Steph Curry (right) lofts a jump shot over Kobe Bryant.

Steph Curry

Steph Curry is an NBA game-changer. The three-point shot dominates today's NBA. Curry is better at shooting it than anyone.

In the 2012–2013 season, Curry made 272 three-pointers. It was the most in NBA history. But he was just getting started! Curry broke his own record in the 2014–2015 season and again in the 2015–2016 season. That season, he made a jaw-dropping 402 long bombs! His sharpshooting helped him win two MVP awards. He also won three NBA titles with the Golden State Warriors.

NBA AVERAGE 3-POINT SHOT ATTEMPTS PER GAME BY SEASON

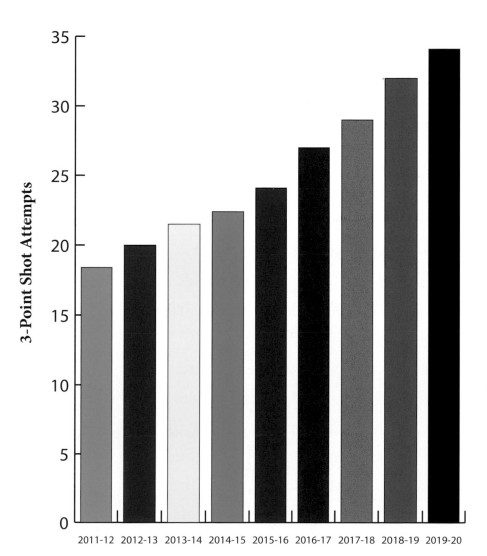

CHAPTER 2

RAISING THE GAME

Some legends just make people stand up and take notice. In the late 1970s, the NBA was struggling. TV ratings were low. Fans didn't seem interested.

Magic Johnson and Larry Bird

Two players changed all of that. Earvin "Magic" Johnson and Larry Bird were **rivals** in college. Once they arrived in the NBA, the league's popularity boomed. Johnson, of the Los Angeles Lakers, was a point guard in a forward's body. He was a wizard with the ball. He made crazy passes with ease. Bird starred on the Boston Celtics. He was a sharpshooting forward with a nose for the ball. The league's popularity surged when they faced off in the NBA Finals. They did this three times, in 1984, 1985, and 1987.

DID YOU KNOW?

The Lakers and Celtics are tied with the most NBA titles in history at 17 each. No other team has more than six!

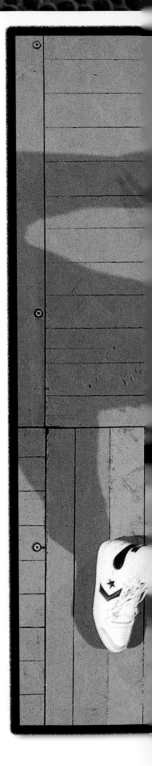

Rivals Larry Bird and Magic Johnson battle for position in a clash between the Celtics and the Lakers.

Jordan celebrates the Bulls championship in 1992. He went on to win six NBA titles.

Michael Jordan

Michael Jordan brought superstardom to a new level. He was a high-flying scoring machine and a shutdown defender. Nobody was better with the game on the line.

Jordan and the Chicago Bulls ruled the 1990s. They won three straight titles from 1991 to 1993. Then, Jordan shocked fans by leaving the NBA. He wanted to try a career in baseball. He came back in 1996 and led Chicago to three more titles. Jordan was an **icon** who was bigger than basketball. Most experts call him the best basketball player of all time.

DR. J

Before Jordan set the league on fire, Julius Erving was the game's most exciting player. His nickname was Dr. J. Fans plastered their walls with posters of his rim-rattling dunks. He made defenders look foolish in the pictures. Fans invented the term *posterizing* to describe it.

Julius Erving was a high-flying dunking machine.

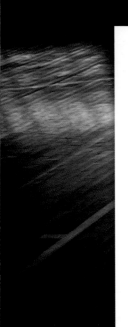

Cynthia Cooper and Lisa Leslie

The NBA had Johnson and Bird. The WNBA had Cynthia Cooper and Lisa Leslie. The rivals were the two biggest stars in the league when it started in 1997. Their skills on the court helped the league grow into what it has become today.

Cooper, of the Houston Comets, could do it all. She was a great passer, shooter, and defender. She led Houston to the first four WNBA championships, from 1997 to 2000.

Lisa Leslie (#9) drives into the lane in a game against the Charlotte Sting.

Cynthia Cooper (front row, left) celebrates with her Houston Comets teammates after their WNBA title in 1997.

Leslie was a physical, athletic center. She was the first WNBA player to dunk in a game. She led the Los Angeles Sparks to championships in 2001 and 2002. The two stars paved the way for a new wave of modern WNBA players.

Bill Russell (#6) drives to the hoop in
a game against the St. Louis Hawks.

CHAPTER 3

LEGENDS OF THE GAME

Some players just seem born to be great. They set the league on fire with their amazing skills.

Bill Russell

When it comes to winning, nobody can match Bill Russell. Russell joined the Celtics in 1956. He was the key to the greatest **dynasty** in NBA history. The 6-foot, 10-inch (208-cm) center was a force under the basket. He was also a great defender.

Russell won 11 NBA titles with Boston. That included eight in a row from 1959 to 1966. He even won two as a player-coach. He served as Boston's head coach and as its center from 1966 to 1969!

DID YOU KNOW?

In 1966, Russell became Boston's head coach. He was the first Black head coach in the NBA. He led Boston to an NBA title in just his second season!

Diana Taurasi

Diana Taurasi is a winner. The 6-foot (182-cm) guard won three championships in college at the University of Connecticut. The Phoenix Mercury chose her with the first pick in the 2004 WNBA Draft. Taurasi didn't disappoint. She led the Mercury to WNBA titles in 2007, 2009, and 2014. And she became the league's all-time highest scorer.

Before becoming a WNBA star, Diana Taurasi (#3) helped the University of Connecticut to three NCAA titles.

UConn's Diana Taurasi (third from left) and teammates celebrate winning the NCAA trophy in 2004 after beating Tennessee for the title.

Taurasi is a big-time playmaker. She can score from inside and outside. She runs the offense and is a great passer. Many people call her the greatest player in WNBA history.

DID YOU KNOW?

Kobe Bryant was one of Taurasi's biggest fans. Bryant, nicknamed the Black Mamba, gave her the nickname The White Mamba. He said it was because she was so good in the clutch.

LeBron James

Most people call Michael Jordan the greatest player in NBA history. But LeBron James is a close second. James was drafted by the Cleveland Cavaliers straight from high school. His power and skill made him a force. He won **Rookie** of the Year in 2004 and became one of the league's best players.

LeBron James throws down a monster dunk in a game against the Detroit Pistons.

James can fill it up from inside and outside. And he's one of the best defenders in the league. The four-time MVP has also won four NBA titles. And he's done it with three different teams!

James (left) celebrates his 2004 Rookie of the Year trophy with Julius Erving.

Candace Parker

At 6 feet, 4 inches (193 cm), Candace Parker is a beast under the basket. She has the moves. She has the size to overpower opponents too. She's a force on the boards and a tough-nosed defender.

Parker came into the WNBA in 2008. She made a big splash. She won Rookie of the Year and MVP in her first season! Parker led the Los Angeles Sparks to the WNBA title in 2016. She also helped the U.S. Olympic team win gold medals in 2008 and 2012. The five-time All-Star remains one of the WNBA's greatest players.

Candace Parker (center) starred for the University of Tennessee before entering the WNBA.

Maya Moore (right) left the WNBA to fight for social justice. Here, she celebrates after helping free an innocent man from prison.

MAYA MOORE: MORE THAN JUST BASKETBALL

Maya Moore is a basketball legend. The Minnesota Lynx chose her with the first pick in the 2011 WNBA Draft. Moore was a key to the team's four WNBA titles over the next seven years.

Moore walked away from the WNBA in 2019. She wanted to focus on **social justice**. Her goal is to help reform the criminal justice system.

GLOSSARY

agility (uh-JIH-luh-tee)—the ability to move quickly and easily

clutch (KLUHCH)—important, game-changing situations

draft (DRAFT)—the system by which pro sports teams select new players

dynasty (DYE-nuh-stee)—a long period of dominance by a team

icon (EYE-kon)—a symbol that stands for something bigger

international (in-tur-NASH-uh-nuhl)—including more than one nation

rival (RYE-vuhl)—team or player with whom one has an especially intense competition

rookie (RUK-ee)—a first-year player

social justice (SOH-shuhl JUHSS-tiss)—the idea that society should treat all people equally and fairly

READ MORE

Jankowski, Matthew. *The Greatest Basketball Players of All Time.* New York: Gareth Stevens Publishing, 2020.

Levit, Joseph. *Basketball's G.O.A.T.: Michael Jordan, LeBron James, and More.* Minneapolis: Lerner Publications, 2020.

Scheff, Matt. *NBA and WNBA Finals.* Minneapolis: Lerner Publications, 2021.

INTERNET SITES

NBA
nba.com/

SIKids Basketball
sikids.com/basketball

WNBA
wnba.com/

INDEX